D0598233

# Miracle

### The True Story of the Wreck of the *Sea Venture*

## by GAIL LANGER KARWOSKI

DISCARD

SANTA CLARA PUBLIC LIBRARY
2635 Homestead Road
Santa Clara, CA 95051

DARBY CREEK PUBLISHING

*For my daughter Geneva,*
*who loves the ocean and the life it nourishes, as much as I do*

This book was made possible, in part, by a grant from the Society of Children's Book Writers and Illustrators.

Published by Darby Creek Publishing,
a division of Oxford Resources, Inc.
7858 Industrial Parkway
Plain City, OH 43064
www.darbycreekpublishing.com

Cataloging-in-Publication

Karwoski, Gail, 1949-
Miracle : the true story of the wreck of the Sea Venture / by Gail Langer Karwoski ; [illustrations by John MacDonald].
    p. ; cm.
ISBN 1-58196-015-8 (lib. bdg.)
Includes bibliographical references and index.—Summary: In the summer of 1609 a fleet of nine ships left England bound for the Jamestown Colony. Days before landfall, the fleet was hit by a hurricane. Four nights later, the flagship, Sea Venture, ran aground on the reefs on Bermuda's northern coast. Miraculously everyone survived. This is their story.
1. Bermuda Islands—History—17th century—Juvenile literature. 2. Sea Venture (Sailing ship) 3. Shipwrecks—Bermuda Islands—Juvenile literature. 4. Bermuda—Discovery and exploration—British—Juvenile literature. 5. Virginia—History—Colonial period, ca. 1600-1775—Juvenile literature. [1. Bermuda Islands—History. 2. Sea Venture (Sailing ship) 3. Shipwrecks—Bermuda Islands. 4. Bermuda—Discovery and exploration—British. 5. Virginia—History—Colonial period, ca. 1600-1775.] I. Title. II. Ill.
F1636 .K37 2004
972.99 dc22
OCLC: 54013010

Text copyright © 2004 by Gail Langer Karwoski
Illustrations on the cover and pages 4, 6, 16, 18, 27, 28, 36, 46, 51 copyright ©2004 by John MacDonald
Design copyright © 2004 by Darby Creek Publishing
Design by Keith Van Norman

All rights reserved. No part of this book may be reproduced or transmitted in any form or by any means, electronic or mechanical, including photocopying, recording, or by an information storage and retrieval system, without permission in writing from the Publisher.

Printed in the United States of America
First printing
2 4 6 8 10 9 7 5 3 1

# Contents

# Introduction

**H**owling winds bore down on the *Sea Venture*. Heaving seas lifted the ship and plunged it into swirling valleys of water. The captain screamed orders, and sailors scurried like agitated ants to grab the whipping sails and fasten them down. The ship blew willy-nilly across the ocean as the hurricane raged. But even more deadly than the storm was the leak that caused the ship's hold to fill with seawater.

The *Sea Venture* was crossing the Atlantic Ocean in the summer of 1609 when the hurricane struck. For a ship to weather both the storm and the leak would take a miracle. The *Sea Venture* got its miracle when it slammed into the coral reef surrounding a small island.

The shipwreck seemed like a disaster, but the passengers and crew made the best of it and learned to live as castaways. Nearly a year later, when they finally resumed their journey and reached their intended destination, they realized that the shipwreck had actually saved them from a far worse disaster!

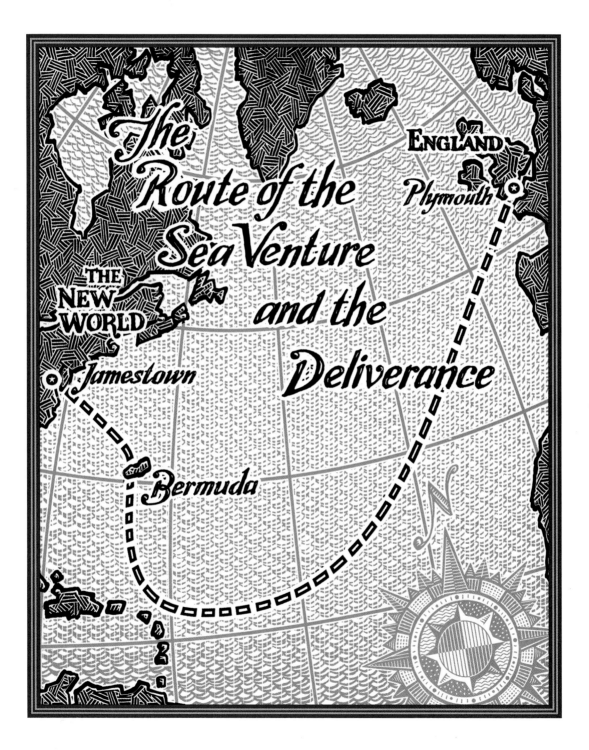

# The Journey

The *Sea Venture* began its journey as one in a fleet of nine ships leaving Plymouth, England, on June 2, 1609. Its destination was the English colony at Jamestown, Virginia. Aboard the nine ships were about five hundred to six hundred people, the largest group of settlers ever sent by England to its first colony in North America. These settlers included women and children. Jamestown had been established two years earlier, but almost all of its previous settlers were men.

In addition to passengers, the ships carried food, ammunition, tools, and other supplies to restock the struggling colony. England had already sent two shipments of supplies to its Virginia colony, but this was the most ambitious.

Seven of the nine ships were full-sized wooden sailing ships. They were named the *Sea Venture*, the *Diamond*, the *Blessing*, the *Falcon*, the *Unitie*, the *Lion*, and the *Swallow*. The remaining two ships were smaller vessels, called pinnaces. Because the larger ships had more sails, they could travel faster. The *Sea Venture* towed one of the pinnaces behind it.

Sir Thomas Gates

Sir George Somers

The *Sea Venture* was a new ship, and this was its first voyage. It was probably the largest ship in the fleet, measuring perhaps as long as one hundred feet. Its hold was spacious enough to carry three hundred large barrels of cargo. The *Sea Venture* probably carried more passengers than any of the other ships in the fleet.

Because the *Sea Venture* was the flagship, it also carried the expedition's leaders. They included two men of high social standing in England: Thomas Gates and George Somers. Both Gates and Somers were knighted, so they were addressed with the special title of "Sir." (Other men of rank were addressed with the titles "Master" or "Captain.") Sir Thomas Gates was going to take over the command of the Jamestown colony. He would act as governor for the next several months or a year, until an even higher-ranking official arrived from England. Sir George Somers was the admiral of the fleet, in charge of all of the ships. Each ship's captain took orders from him. If major decisions needed to be made during the ocean crossing, Admiral Somers would have the final say.

The *Sea Venture*'s captain was Christopher Newport. He had plenty of experience sailing across the Atlantic Ocean to North America. Captain Newport was about forty-nine years old and "one of the greatest of England's sea-captains" when the *Sea Venture* set sail. This was the fourth time he had been in charge of a ship going to the Jamestown colony. He had been the commander of the original fleet that brought the first group of settlers to Jamestown in 1607, and he had returned to the colony with the previous supply ships.

## Captain Christopher Newport

By the time he led fleets to Virginia, Newport already had had a long and colorful history at sea. During most of his career, he sailed in the Caribbean as a *privateer*—a pirate employed by British businessmen to raid Spanish ships and towns! Before he was thirty, Newport became the captain of a ship and, that same year, lost his right arm during the capture of two Mexican treasure ships. Two years later, his fleet captured the *Madre de Dios*, one of the richest Spanish ships ever taken by English privateers.

Eventually, Newport became one of the British navy's principal masters and a member of Virginia's governing council. The Virginia town of Newport News was probably named in his honor.

Newport led a total of five voyages to Jamestown in five years. Then he joined the East India Company, commanded three voyages to Southeast Asia and India, and rose to the rank of Admiral. In 1617, after the third Asian voyage, Christopher Newport died in Indonesia. One historian wrote that he "lived on the ocean; he died on the ocean; the ocean is his tomb, and his admirable monument."

Bronze statue of Captain Christopher Newport by sculptor Jon Hair.
© Copyright 2003 Jon Hair Studio of Fine Art LLC. All Rights Reserved.

During the entire month of June and most of July, the fleet enjoyed a smooth and uneventful voyage. The sailors kept within sight of each other's ships as they sailed. On July 23rd, they were heading west, somewhere between 26°N and 30°N latitude. Captain Newport expected to reach Virginia in seven or eight days at the most.

But clouds began to gather, and the wind picked up. William Strachey, a passenger on the *Sea Venture*, later wrote about the hurricane that hit their ship. He called it "a dreadful storm and hideous." Strachey reported that the winds, which were coming from the northeast, "beat all light from heaven." Huge waves that "swelled above the clouds" tossed the ships up and down. Strachey wrote that rain came down so hard that "the waters like whole rivers did flood in the air."

## Why didn't ships cross the Atlantic Ocean in a straight line?

In the early seventeenth century, large ships were powered by the wind. The captains going from Europe to the New World chose their routes according to the way the trade winds blew. When the ships set sail, they headed south. They turned west when they neared the Canary Islands, off the coast of Africa. Traced on a map, their route looks like an arc, dipping almost as far south as the equator. It took about two months to make the crossing.

NORTH ATLANTIC TRADE WINDS

NORTH AMERICA

EUROPE

AFRICA

SOUTH AMERICA

## Why didn't sailing ships tip over?

Heavy stones, called *ballast*, lined the floor of a ship's hold. Ballast weighted the ship's bottom to keep it upright on the rolling surface of the ocean. Cargo was stored on top of the ballast. If a ship carried lots of heavy cargo, then less ballast was needed. Without any ballast, a ship would be top-heavy and flop onto its side. The more masts and rigging that a sailing ship had on deck, the more ballast had to be piled in its bottom.

To prevent the ship from smashing into the towed pinnace, the crew of the *Sea Venture* cut the smaller ship loose. In the stormy darkness, the mariners lost sight of the rest of the fleet. Suddenly, their orderly expedition turned into a battle, a fight against a storm.

Admiral Somers raced to the poop deck, the raised deck at the rear of the ship. From this position, he directed the sailor who was steering the ship with a lever called the whipstaff. Somers knew how important it was to keep the wind from hitting the ship broadside. If its side was battered by powerful winds, a wooden ship could capsize and be swallowed by the waves. Somers probably decided to let the *Sea Venture* "run with the winds"—to let the storm push the ship from behind.

The storm hammered the *Sea Venture*. Below deck, terrified passengers clutched the wooden beams. Trunks worked loose from the ropes that lashed them and careened across the floor. Children screamed in terror, babies wailed, and grown men and women prayed.

Then the unthinkable happened: The *Sea Venture* began to leak! Like all of the ships of the period, she was made of wood. A leak was always a concern. But this ship was brand-new, and nobody expected her to leak.

Both sailors and passengers were horrified when they realized water was filling the hold, the lowest level of the ship. By the time the *Sea Venture*'s leak was discovered, seawater had already formed a pond. Five feet of water was standing in the hold!

The sailors immediately started the pumps and began to search for the leak. The storm had blotted out the sun, so the men held candles in order to see. During the next few hours, they examined every inch of the ship. They found small cracks where water was seeping in and patched these with whatever they could find, including pieces of beef! But they never found the main source of the leak.

Meanwhile, water was sloshing into the bread room, a small storage area where hard-baked biscuits, called hardtack, were kept. A large quantity of hardtack was carried on long voyages, enough to feed both passengers and the crew. Floating in the seawater, the biscuits dissolved into soggy mush, and as the

## How did wooden ships keep water out?

Ship builders pounded a material called *oakum*, made of hemp fibers from worn-out ropes, into the seams between the wooden planks. Then these seams were covered with hot pitch, a mixture of tar and resin. The bottom of the ship's hull, below the water level, was also painted with the sealer. Periodically, a ship had to be hauled out of the water so the waterproofing could be reapplied.

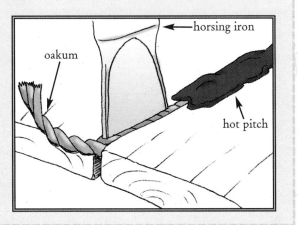

pumps drained out the water, the mush was sucked in. It clogged the pumps. The pond in the hold of the ship rose to nearly ten feet deep—and the water continued to pour in.

As soon as Gates saw the water in the hold, he enlisted the passengers' help to rescue the ship. He assigned all of the male passengers to work with sailors in one of three companies: one working under the forecastle in the front of the ship; one in the waist, or middle section; and one near the stern, or back.

The companies opened the hatches leading down to the hold, and the men formed human chains to pass buckets, casks, and kettles of water up to the deck to be dumped overboard. Each man worked in one-hour shifts: one hour working and one hour resting. Strachey estimated that the three companies emptied one hundred tons of water out of the ship every four hours. Yet, the water in the ship's hold continued to rise.

The storm raged on. Working around the clock, aristocrats took their turn beside common laborers. Even Sir Thomas Gates and Admiral Somers took turns, inspiring the others to keep working. The men stood in sloshing seawater as they pumped and bailed out water. Shivering with cold, many of them stripped off their sopping clothes. The brine made their skin shrivel, and salt spray stung their eyes.

For three days and four nights, with no food and little to drink, the men labored. Day blurred into night. The ship seemed to be sailing into a black nowhere—far from its companion ships—out of time and place. Water spilled over the rails and seeped in through the ship's seams. With trembling, slippery hands, passengers and sailors bailed and patched, pumped and poured. Yet the winds blew, the sea heaved, and water filled the hold. The men became dazed with exhaustion.

Suddenly, an enormous swell broke over the stern of the ship. Water hit the *Sea Venture* with such force that the breath was knocked out of the men on deck. The helmsman was swept off his feet, and the whipstaff lever ripped out of his hand. When he tried to grab the whipstaff, it slipped from his hands and banged into him, knocking him from one side of the ship to the other until his body was bruised from head to legs. The ship pitched wildly from side to side. Finally, another crewmember managed to grab hold of the whipstaff and steady the vessel.

Meanwhile, below deck, the passengers saw a sudden flood of water pouring in and felt the wild lurching of the ship. They thought the *Sea Venture* was sinking! Men and women began to say their last prayers. Gates struggled to climb through the hatch so he could die under the open sky.

But the *Sea Venture* was not sinking—not yet.

## A Strange Sight at Night

On the fourth night of the storm, Admiral Somers thought he saw a flame shooting out of the top of the mast. As he stared at it, the light flickered like a tiny star. It danced around the mast and darted from sail to sail. Somers called the others to see this strange sight, which he recognized as an electrical discharge called St. Elmo's fire. (St. Elmo was the patron saint of sailors.)

Sailors sometimes saw this phenomenon during dark nights of thunderstorms. Some superstitious sailors believed it was an evil omen, but others thought it foretold the end of the storm.

The strange light continued to flicker around the *Sea Venture's* mast for three or four hours, then disappeared as morning approached.

© National Oceanic and Atmospheric Administration

At the start of the storm, the crew tied the sails around the masts to keep them from filling with wind. Even so, the *Sea Venture* did not remain in one spot. Whipped by the winds and tossed by the seas, the ship careened across miles of ocean, shifting from north to northeast to west. Although the admiral knew the ship was moving, he could not steer toward Virginia. All he could do was continue to "run with the waves," letting the storm push the *Sea Venture* from behind.

With all the water in its hold, the ship was dangerously bottom-heavy. It rolled in the heavy seas, and its cargo shifted dangerously to starboard, the right side of the ship. This caused the *Sea Venture* to dip nearly sideways, so the sailors hurried to lighten that side of the ship. Desperately, men hauled up heavy chests and threw them overboard. Passengers watched trunks full of clothing, blankets, pots, and tools splash into the wild waves. Sailors also tossed

Items recovered from the *Sea Venture*
©Dr. Jonathan Adams/Sea Venture Trust

out casks of beer, wine, cider, oil, and vinegar. Everybody knew these supplies would be vitally important to the colony's survival in the new land, but the threat from the sea was immediate and urgent.

The storm hit the *Sea Venture* on Monday, according to Strachey's account. By first light on Friday, many of the passengers were ready to give up. Convinced they were going to drown anyway, they were tired of bailing. They talked about letting the ship fill with water and sink. But Admiral Somers remained on deck, refusing to give up.

In mid-morning, the sky began to lighten. Most of the men were so worn out that they hardly noticed the change in the sky. They simply crawled into corners and fell asleep as soon as they finished their hour-long work shifts.

Suddenly, Admiral Somers spotted a coast emerging from the clouds. "Land!" he cried.

Passengers shook off their stupor and pulled themselves to their feet. They gaped at the horizon. Land? Yes, they could see land! They saw trees on a shore. They saw branches blowing in the wind.

The boatswain threw the sounding lead into the water to determine how close the ship was to the shore. The first time he sounded, he read the water depth at thirteen fathoms. A few minutes later, he sounded and came up with seven fathoms. The third time, he read four fathoms. The *Sea Venture* was moving into the shallow water within a mile of shore!

Although the water was somewhat calmer near land than out in the open ocean, it was too turbulent to hold the ship steady at anchor. The captain and admiral decided their only chance was to run the *Sea Venture* aground as close to shore as possible.

With a terrible grinding noise, the ship slammed into a coral reef and lurched to a standstill. It wedged on rocks about three-quarters of a mile from shore. Frantically, passengers scrambled into rowboats and sailors pulled for shore. As the rowboats neared the beach, load after load of settlers tumbled into the surf and waded onto solid ground. The sailors quickly rowed back to collect more passengers. Everybody expected the *Sea Venture* to crack and break into pieces at any moment.

On July 28, 1609, the first and only voyage of the *Sea Venture* ended abruptly on the reefs surrounding an island in the Atlantic. Miraculously, every passenger and crewmember—about 150 people in all—managed to reach the shore. Not a single soul was lost during the entire ordeal. Even the ship's dog had survived!

## What is a sounding lead?

Before modern systems of sonar were invented, a sailor would toss a *sounding lead* overboard to determine the depth of the ocean below his ship. The sailor knew that the closer the ship came to land, the shallower the ocean would become.

How did a sounding lead work? A hollow iron weight filled with a waxy substance called tallow was tied to the end of a rope. Knots or bits of colored cloth were tied along the rope every fathom or so. (A fathom is about six feet.) By counting the knots, a sailor could judge the ocean's depth. When the weight scraped the sandy bottom, bits of sand stuck to the tallow. If the sounding lead came up sandy, the sailor knew it had touched the sea floor. Land was not far away.

# Enchanted Islands

With the passengers safe on shore, the sailors rushed back to the *Sea Venture* to save whatever they could. They were able to salvage food, blankets, cloth, cooking pots, earthenware containers, lanterns, candles, guns, ammunition, and swords—most of the ship's remaining cargo. Of course, many supplies had already been tossed overboard during the storm.

In addition to cargo, the sailors hauled tools and gear off the ship. They grabbed carpenter's tools, sail-maker's equipment, navigator's instruments, and ropes. They even stripped off parts of the ship, ripping down masts, sails, rigging, doors, hatches, planks, and iron fittings. All they left to the sea was the shell of the ruined ship.

What did the passengers do while the mariners rowed back and forth to empty the ship? There is no record. Some might have been so overcome with emotion that they knelt to kiss the solid ground. Mothers and fathers probably wept as they hugged their children. The clergyman, Reverend Richard Bucke, probably called his flock together to say a prayer of thanks to the Almighty for delivering them from death. The sun's warm rays must have felt like a blessing upon their weary shoulders. What a miracle this landfall was!

Any celebration would have been brief, though, because there was much work to do. Passengers needed to drag trunks, roll barrels, and carry crates from the shore to higher ground. The women probably opened the chests and spread out blankets and other possessions to let them dry in the sun. The men unpacked the guns, then dried and oiled the iron so rust would not spoil the firing mechanisms. As the shipwrecked colonists worked, their sea-soaked clothes would have dried out, the salt making the clothing feel stiff against their arms and legs.

Children were expected to help with the work. They were probably told to gather wood for fires. After spending nearly two months on a crowded, stinky ship, the children must have skipped merrily across the shoreline, delighted by the clean-smelling air and open space. As they stooped to pick up pieces of driftwood, they probably giggled at the touch of wet seaweed under bare toes.

During the long days and nights of the storm, it had been impossible to cook on the ship. All of the ship's biscuit had been destroyed. Much of the dried beans and grain would have been moldy and ruined from the dampness. The sailors had used the salted meat to patch leaks in the ship's seams.

After directing the sailors' work, Admiral Somers started fishing. A passenger named Sylvester Jourdain recorded that "in half an hour he took so many great fishes with hooks as did suffice the whole company one day."

When the passengers and crew finally sat down to share a hearty meal of cooked fish, they rejoiced at their good fortune. But they would have been nervous, too. Why? Because they knew they were in Bermuda.

As soon as Admiral Somers and Captain Newport sighted land, they would have used the ship's navigational instruments to determine their location. All sea-going men of the seventeenth century had heard of Bermuda—and they were terrified of the place.

In fact, Bermuda had such a notorious reputation that it was called the Devil's Islands! According to Jourdain, the islands of Bermuda were thought to be an "enchanted place, affording nothing but gusts, storms, and foul weather, which made every navigator and mariner avoid them." Strachey, who had written such a powerful account of the hurricane, said that Bermuda was "feared and avoided of all sea travelers alive above any other place in the world."

Although Europeans had never settled on these uninhabited shores, Bermuda was drawn on the maps of the period. The first map that contained "la Bermuda" was published nearly a century earlier, in 1511. The name "Bermuda" came from the Spanish ship captain, Juan de Bermudez, who sailed near the islands in his ship, *La Garza* (which means "the heron"), around 1505.

A portion of Map of the Americas (1562) by Diego Gutiérrez showing Bermuda surrounded by sea monsters and a shipwreck.

In the sixteenth and early seventeenth centuries, mariners knew that Bermuda was located about six hundred miles east of Chesapeake Bay—and they carefully avoided the place.

Why were sailors afraid to land at Bermuda? The islands are surrounded by coral reefs. These are the most northern coral reefs in the world, and they may have surprised the earliest navigators. Coral reefs are sharp enough to rip open the hull of a ship. When captains tried to land in an emergency, such as during a storm, their ships almost always were dashed to bits, and the crews drowned in the rough seas.

Over the years, a few fortunate sailors had been washed ashore after their ships were wrecked. These men reached the islands badly shaken by their ordeal at sea. They were further unnerved by Bermuda's birds. Several types of seabirds came to Bermuda to nest. Since there were no natural predators on the islands, the birds had no fear of people. By day, long-tailed tropic birds would hover in the air, watching people. These birds had a habit of swooping at anyone standing on the cliffs, which must have scared the castaways.

Far more frightening were the nocturnal birds. The cahows, also called Bermuda petrels, were abundant in the fall, when they came to nest on the sandy beaches. Unafraid of people, these birds would fly right up to sailors in the darkness and land on their arms, heads, and shoulders.

Another common seabird in Bermuda was the pimli-co, or Audubon's shearwater. As these birds flew, they let out whistled screams that made sailors think of witches

cahow

laughing. Some sailors thought the birds were crying the Spanish words, *"dice-lo, dicelo,"* meaning "tell it, tell it." Thinking the birds were evil spirits come to harass them, the sailors beat them off in a panic and ran into the underbrush to hide. After this nerve-wracking welcome, the castaways wanted nothing but to escape from the islands. Those who did escape spread the word that Bermuda was haunted by supernatural forces.

Fortunately, when the passengers and crew from the *Sea Venture* landed on Bermuda's shore, the nocturnal seabirds were not nesting. Strachey reported that the settlers did not see any of these birds until November.

## What is the Bermuda Triangle?

The Bermuda Triangle, also known as the Devil's Triangle, is an imaginary triangle that runs from Bermuda to Miami, Florida, to Puerto Rico. The area within this triangle has a fearsome reputation, based on the mysterious disappearances of ships and airplanes. Some people claim that a higher-than-normal number of plane crashes and shipwrecks have happened there. Adding to the mystery is the fact that searchers have sometimes found neither bodies nor debris from the wreckage. The most famous incident happened during World War II when a squadron of five bomber planes vanished in the Triangle.

Some people have speculated that the Bermuda Triangle is a supernatural "port" to another dimension—or even that it is under the control of aliens! Scientists believe such ideas are nonsense, and instead explain that the lost ships and planes could have been swept away by unexpected storms and ocean currents.

The *Sea Venture* had slammed into the coral reef off the northeastern end of Bermuda, on the "eye of the fish hook," which today is known as St. George's Island. Most of that shoreline was rocky, with a stretch of mangrove swamps and a short expanse of sandy beach. Inland, a forest blanketed the island.

As soon as the tasks of landing were done, the castaways ventured into the forest to round up the ship's hogs, which had run off in search of food. The *Sea Venture*, like most ships of its period, carried hogs as an emergency food source. When settlers reached their destination, the hogs were to be raised as livestock.

In the forest, the castaways discovered a dense expanse of trees. At the edge of the forest, evergreen cedar trees grew, their thick, brown trunks twisted into braids by the strong sea winds. These cedars had small, green needles growing on branches that curved up toward the sky. They reached heights of fifteen to twenty feet.

## Beautiful Bermuda

The islands of Bermuda were formed by an ancient volcano on the sea floor. Over centuries, the volcanic material was capped by a 250-foot-thick layer of limestone, deposited by coral.

Bermuda has six larger islands and more than one hundred and fifty smaller islands. These lie in a curve, like a slender chain of beads. The shape of this chain is often compared to a fishhook. From the "eye" at the northeast tip to the fishhook's "point" in the southwest, Bermuda measures about twenty-one miles long. At its widest, it is five miles across.

Palmettos grew about as tall as the cedars, but the bark on their grayish trunks seemed to wind around the tree in circular ribbons. Unlike the cedars, palmetto trees didn't resemble any of the trees that grew in England. The palmetto leaves were huge, shaggy, and fan-shaped.

As they tramped along the forest floor, the settlers probably noticed the spongy, reddish-brown soil. They saw thick clumps of grasses in the clearings and lacy ferns in shady spots. Plants were thriving in the island's warm, humid air.

Welcomed by the cheerful song of Bermuda's white-eyed vireo, the settlers wandered deeper into the forest. Looking up into the treetops, they may not have spotted the drab-colored vireos, but they surely would have noticed flashes of gorgeous blue as eastern bluebirds darted from branch to branch. The sounds of the men pushing through the brush would have disturbed the catbirds feeding on berries. As these seven- to eight-inch black birds flew out of the bushes, they would have made a mew-like cry—the sound that gives them their name. Crows, pecking at the ground, would have scattered and flown onto nearby branches. Glancing at the sky, the men might have noticed hawks wheeling through the clouds.

The men probably scanned the ground for snakes— but they saw none. The only type of land reptile on Bermuda when the settlers arrived was a small lizard, called the Bermuda rock lizard, or skink. The immature lizards were (and are) easiest to spot, because their bodies are striped

skink

25

black, white, and tan, and their tails are bright blue. Adult skinks have shiny gray bodies and grow to about six inches long.

The settlers' nerves were still strained from their ordeal at sea. As they herded the ship's hogs, they must have jumped when they heard a large creature crash through the underbrush. It was a huge wild boar! It had probably come to investigate the sows from the ship's stock.

That evening, one of the sailors had an idea. He thought he could capture the boar by lying down in the midst of the ship's sows. When the boar approached, the sailor gently rubbed the boar's side, then slid a loop of rope under its hind leg. The rope was tied in a slipknot, and it tightened as soon as the boar tried to run off.

Of course, the settlers were delighted to find wild hogs on the island. These animals would provide a fine source of fresh meat.

As dusk set in, the settlers must have noticed that they weren't bothered by insects, either in the forest or on the shore. What a pleasant surprise—to be free of the biting and buzzing pests that are usually troublesome in warm

## Why were hogs living on Bermuda?

Almost certainly, earlier Europeans had brought the swine aboard their ships. The hogs may have swum to shore from ships wrecked on the reefs—or, more likely, they were put overboard on purpose by ships passing close to the reefs. Mariners probably hoped the hogs would swim to shore and breed on the islands, where they would provide meat for any castaways who might land there later.

climates! In fact, the settlers soon discovered that few gnats, mosquitoes, flies, or beetles lived on Bermuda. Except for the large dragonflies in the islands' mangrove swamps, and the cicadas on the cedar trees, the islands had almost no insect life. When darkness closed upon the settlers, they listened to the familiar sound of owls hooting and were reminded of their home in England.

In the weeks and months to come, the settlers changed their opinion of Bermuda. Jourdain decided it was "the richest, healthfullest, and pleasing land . . . as ever man set foot on." The islands were not haunted or threatening. In fact, Bermuda provided almost everything that the castaways needed: pleasant weather, a variety of foods, and materials to build shelter. Eventually, many of the passengers became so fond of the place that they wanted to stay instead of continuing their journey to Jamestown.

JAMESTOWN, 1607

# Summer and Autumn, 1609

The passengers and crew settled comfortably into life on their island home—but Sir Thomas Gates was worried. Gates knew he was the hope of Jamestown, the English colony that had been plagued with problems. Since founding Jamestown in 1607, its settlers had faced severe food shortages, disease, and devastating Indian attacks. English investors believed Jamestown could succeed, but only with strong, effective leadership.

Gates was supposed to take command of Jamestown as soon as the *Sea Venture* arrived. Now his arrival was delayed. Indeed, how could the Virginia colonists know whether he would be arriving at all? What would happen to Jamestown without new leadership?

Gates decided it was critical to send word of his whereabouts to Jamestown. He was also eager to let the other Englishmen know his shipmates were alive and in need of rescue. So he and Admiral Somers ordered sailors to remodel the *Sea Venture*'s longboat to withstand an ocean voyage.

Using wooden hatch covers from the wrecked ship, the sailors enclosed the large rowboat's open deck. They added a mast and sails. Then they packed supplies of food and water to last several weeks. Gates wrote letters appointing another English gentleman as interim leader, and he placed his letters in a watertight container aboard the remodeled boat.

## Sir Thomas Gates

Sir Thomas Gates was born in the town of Colyford, in Devonshire, England, in 1559. He fought in the Dutch wars and sailed on Drake's voyage to the Caribbean in 1585. Gates was knighted at the age of twenty-seven.

Sir Thomas Gates was about fifty years old and an experienced military leader when the *Sea Venture* set sail. England's King James II had chosen him to be the Jamestown colony's first governor because a strong leader was needed to organize and motivate the colonists. By the time Gates reached Jamestown in 1610, Lord De La Warr was already en route from England to assume command of the colony. Gates remained at the colony for only two months before returning to England.

The following year, Sir Thomas Gates set sail for Virginia again, this time taking his wife and five children. His wife died aboard ship, but the rest of the family safely reached Jamestown, where Gates served as governor for three years. In 1619, a prominent English leader said that Gates's "wisdom, industry, and valor . . . had laid the foundation" for the Virginia colony's prosperity.

Gates left Jamestown in 1614 and later served on the king's council, helping to oversee the new British colony in New England—the Plymouth colony—in 1620. Soon after, he journeyed to the East Indies, where he died in 1621.

Sir Thomas Gates

Volunteers were needed for the six-hundred-mile voyage. Captain Newport's first mate, Henry Ravens, had

shallop (longboat)
©Plimoth Plantation, Plymouth, Massachusetts www.plimoth.org

some skill as a pilot. He agreed to head the longboat's crew. Thomas Whittingham also volunteered for the dangerous assignment. Whittingham was the cape merchant, the sailor in charge of the *Sea Venture*'s supplies. Six other sailors joined the rescue party.

By the end of August, the longboat was ready. Ravens promised that if he survived the journey, he would return immediately with a ship. He expected to reach Jamestown and be back in a month or so.

The small crew began its journey on Monday, August 28, 1609. The following Wednesday night, the longboat returned. Ravens had attempted to sail in a southwesterly direction away from the islands, but he could not find a channel through Bermuda's reefs. He set out again two days later, on Friday, September 1st, and this time he headed southeast. By backtracking along the route that the *Sea Venture* had taken to Bermuda, Ravens was finally able to wind his way clear of the reefs.

A few weeks later, Somers began looking for Ravens's ship. The admiral posted a round-the-clock watch. He directed men to build a signal fire on high ground along the coast so Bermuda would be easier to see from a ship at sea.

Meanwhile, the settlers attended to the daily tasks of living. Bermuda's weather was pleasantly warm when they arrived in July. It remained mostly sunny and warm throughout August, September, and into October, with occasional strong thunderstorms that brought heavy winds and drenching rains.

Needing housing right away, the Englishmen probably built open-sided structures—roofs supported by four posts cut from cedar trunks. During the summer rains, the castaways quickly discovered that the broad, stiff leaves of palmetto trees made excellent umbrellas—water slid right off the smooth surface of the leaves. The settlers wove the palmetto leaves into roofs on their houses.

The colonists welcomed the rain as their best source for drinking water. Although the men had searched the islands for rivers or springs, they did not find any. Their attempts to dig wells didn't succeed, either, because they found only saltwater below ground. So they set out barrels and dug shallow pits to collect rain. (Later, they found flat areas at the base of hills where rainwater collected in shallow pools.)

Berries were a ready source of food. Both palmetto and cedar trees produced edible berries. The berries of the palmetto

## Bermuda's Palmetto Tree

Palmetto trees provided both shelter and food for the castaways. Palmettos have a "head" of soft material, weighing about twenty pounds, which grows at the top of their trunks. When the settlers ate these heads raw, they compared the taste to melons. The women also boiled the palmetto heads and used them like cabbages.

trees grew as large as plums. When they were green, the women cooked them over outdoor cooking fires, but in December, when the berries ripened, the settlers ate them soft and sweet right off the tree. The settlers also discovered that the fruit of prickly pear cactus, which grew on the islands' rocks, produced a juice that tasted like mulberries. They ate the pears both raw and baked.

palmetto berries

Fish remained a major part of the settlers' diet. At first, the fish were so abundant that the men refused to wade into the water because they feared the fish would bite them. After a while the colonists' cooking fires and unfamiliar activities scared the fish away from the beach. Needing a way to catch enough fish to eat, the settlers wove a large net. Strachey reported taking "five thousand of small and great fish at one hale" when they trawled their net through the shallows.

The men also built a small, flat-bottomed boat from cedar wood. Out farther from shore, they caught "excellent angelfish, salmon, peal, bonitos, stingray, cavally, snappers, hogfish, sharks, dogfish, pilchards, mullets, and rockfish." In fact, the settlers caught far more fish than they could eat fresh. So they dried and salted fish for later use.

In addition to fish, the settlers turned over rocks to collect shellfish, such as oysters, whelks, and other crustaceans. Bermuda's crayfish grew as large as lobsters. Crabs were also abundant.

The islands of Bermuda were the nesting grounds for many species of birds—seabirds, such as cahows, shearwaters, tropic birds, and terns; marsh

birds, such as heron, egrets, ducks, and moorhens; and land birds, such as eastern bluebirds, catbirds, crows, and vireos. The birds were plentiful and unafraid of people. Hunters learned they could attract birds by whistling, singing, or even laughing. When the curious birds came close, the men struck at them with sticks or simply grabbed them with bare hands. So many birds could be captured this way that hunters began releasing any small or light ones and kept only the meatiest to roast.

heron

The birds provided eggs as well as meat. Jourdain described a bird the size of a pigeon that laid eggs as large as hen eggs. He wrote that these birds had no fear of humans and continued to deposit their eggs in the sand even as the men walked among them. The settlers could catch at least a thousand of these birds in three hours, and they could gather as many eggs in a morning.

During the dark nights of November and December, the colonists encountered the nocturnal cahows and shearwaters, the birds that had terrified earlier castaways. Strachey wrote that these birds "would come forth, but not fly far from home, and hovering in the air and over the sea, made a strange hollow and harsh howling." The seabirds were so abundant that Strachey reported he could capture three hundred of them in an hour.

Birds were not the only source of meat. The settlers also hunted the wild hogs that roamed the forests. The ship's dog proved helpful during these hunts. The dog chased a hog until it was cornered, and then the hunters moved in to capture it alive. The men captured thirty to fifty hogs per week, kept them in pens, and fed them cedar berries and palmetto berries. With livestock in their pens, the settlers had a steady supply of protein, even when it was too stormy to fish.

Toward the end of October, Bermuda's weather turned windy and raw. In spite of the rain and chilly winds, the settlers kept watching for Henry Ravens's return. Gates assigned shifts of men to keep the signal fire burning continuously. During daylight, the men scanned the surface of the endless blue-green water. All night long, they stoked the fire and listened for the flapping of sails.

They never spotted the English ship returning to pick them up. They didn't spot any other ships, either. As the weeks wore on, their hope for rescue began to fade. At the end of November, they finally gave up. If a ship had set sail from Jamestown, it would have reached Bermuda by this time. Either the longboat was lost at sea or Ravens had been unable to return with a rescue ship. With heavy hearts, the settlers realized they were on their own.

## Please Pass the Salt

Salt was important to the settlers, who used it to preserve fish and meat, as well as to season food. When the supply of salt ran out, Sir Gates set up a salt-making operation. The settlers built a small hut near the shore, and Gates assigned men to work in shifts. The workers filled three or four pots with seawater and set these on fires to boil off the liquid. After the water evaporated, the men collected the salt that remained.

# Winter Rebellions

As the sudden thunderstorms of summer became less frequent and autumn set in, cooler temperatures arrived. Gradually, daylight shortened to about ten hours per day. Before long, the winter winds blew hard, and the damp air made a person feel chilled to the bone. Even so, the settlers didn't complain. At least the islands did not get snow or ice.

Bermuda offered a wealth of resources, but the settlers' days were by no means leisurely. They had to work from morning until night—and the work was strenuous. Men felled trees, hunted and fished, stood guard at camp, and took turns at the salt-making operation. Winter weather forced them to build walls for their open dwellings. Women lugged buckets of water, prepared meals, preserved meat and fish, mended clothing, and helped with the building projects. Even children worked hard gathering firewood, collecting oysters and crayfish, weaving nets, and assisting grownups with various chores.

As governor, Sir Thomas Gates was in charge of the settlement on St. George's Island. He organized a work schedule and made sure each man took his turn at common tasks, such as salt-making, guarding the settlement, and building a storehouse to keep food and supplies dry. Gates also considered the group's future. He knew that a passing ship was unlikely to find them on Bermuda. The settlers would have to build their own ship—and rescue themselves. Already working hard from sunup to sundown, some of the settlers were less than eager to take on the additional backbreaking work of building a wooden ship.

Some shipbuilding actually had begun as soon as the longboat was launched in August. Even if Ravens did manage to return, Gates knew they would also need more than one ship. The settlers had arrived on the *Sea Venture*, which was a very large ship. There were too many castaways to crowd aboard one smaller ship for the long voyage to Virginia.

Soon after Ravens had departed in his longboat, Gates assigned men to work under Richard Furbusher, the *Sea Venture*'s shipwright. Furbusher used wood salvaged from the wreck itself to construct a new ship, which would be called the *Deliverance*.

## How did they build houses?

In Jamestown, English settlers built their houses using the "wattle and daub" method, and this is probably the same method that was used by the settlers in Bermuda. Walls were erected by pounding wooden posts into the ground, every two feet or so, to form a row. Then the men wove flexible branches between the upright posts ("wattle") and filled in the spaces with a mixture of mud, clay, and animal hair ("daub").

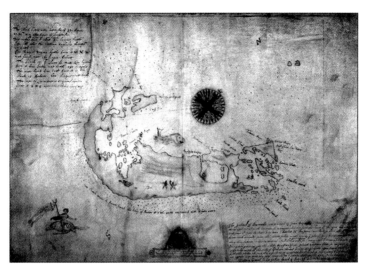

Somers' Map
Bermuda National Trust Collection, Bermuda Archives: PA 377

During autumn, while the watch was still being kept for Ravens's crew, Admiral Somers took charge of the colony's hunting and fishing needs. He also rowed a small boat around the islands and drew the first accurate map of the area.

In late November, after they had abandoned the watch for a rescue ship, Gates and Somers had a meeting. Because the *Deliverance* was not going to be large enough to carry their entire party to Jamestown, they had to come up with a solution. Should they leave behind some of the settlers—or build a second ship?

Admiral Somers offered to supervise the construction of a second vessel, to be called the *Patience*, from Bermuda's native cedar. He took two of the company's four carpenters and a workforce of twenty able men and located his shipbuilding project on Bermuda's largest island, where there was an ample supply of cedar.

# Sir George Somers

Admiral George Somers was fifty-five years old when he sailed on the *Sea Venture*. People who knew him said he was "a lamb on the land, so patient that few could anger him," but when he was in command of a ship, his personality changed to that of "a lion at sea, so passionate that few could please him."

He was born in the town of Lyme Regis, in Dorset, England, in 1554 to a middle-class—not wealthy—family. He married a woman from the same town and social class. By the time Somers was thirty-three years old, he was a prosperous landowner. Just how did he earn his fortune? He got his money as a buccaneer—a polite term for a pirate! In those days, it was an accepted practice for English ships to seize Spanish ships and sell their cargo for profit.

In 1595, Somers gained a reputation for heroism during the capture of a Spanish city in Venezuela. Two years later, he commanded a ship returning from the Azores (islands in the north Atlantic Ocean, near Portugal)—in a fleet led by Sir Walter Raleigh—and managed to save his ship from a terrible storm. To honor his deeds, Somers was knighted in 1603. He became a member of the English government, representing Lyme Regis in Parliament during 1603 and 1604. The next year he became the town's mayor.

Somers played an important part in the English company that colonized Virginia. He helped organize and finance the fleet of nine ships that went to Jamestown in 1609. He believed so strongly in the project that he even mortgaged one of his properties to get enough money.

Considered the "Father of Bermuda," Somers loved the islands, which he described at "the most plentiful place that ever I came to for fish, hogs, and fowl." He died in Bermuda in November 1610, after a strenuous voyage to gather food for the Jamestown colony.

Among Somers's workers was a sailor named Robert Waters, known for his quick, violent temper. Soon after they had arrived in Bermuda, Waters had been involved in a fatal brawl with another sailor. In that incident, Waters struck the other sailor with a shovel and killed him. For this crime, Waters was condemned to be hanged, but the other sailors released Waters and concealed him in the woods. Somers negotiated his pardon by pleading with Gates that Waters had given valuable service aboard ship.

Soon, however, Waters became involved in another crime—an organized rebellion against shipbuilding—a more serious matter. The first of three such rebellions was discovered on September 1, 1609. Gates learned that six men had made a secret pact to refuse any task involving the construction of the ship. "Why should we?" these men reasoned. "Bermuda is a fine place to live, so why work extra hours to build a ship to go to Virginia? There, the colonists have to struggle to find enough food."

These six men formed a conspiracy and tried to influence others, like the blacksmith and one of the carpenters. When Gates found out about the scheme, he condemned the six men to exile. John Want, the head of this conspiracy, and his five followers were taken to another of Bermuda's islands and left there. (Among Want's co-conspirators was Christopher Carter, who would soon be involved in another insurrection.)

Their exile did not last long. The six men hated being isolated, so they begged Gates's forgiveness. He pardoned them and allowed them to return to the settlement at St. George's Island.

The second rebellion surfaced in January. Two men claimed that Stephen Hopkins had encouraged them to disobey Gates's orders. The settlers were shocked to learn of Hopkins's treason. He had been considered a man of good conscience: He had a wife and children in England, and he was so religious that he served as clerk to Minister Bucke at Sunday services.

Gates ordered his men to arrest Hopkins and put him in manacles. At a public trial, Hopkins's crime was read before the entire assembly. Hopkins denied the charges, but when he was found guilty and sentenced to death, he admitted his crime and begged for mercy. He pleaded that his death would mean ruin for his family. Captain Newport, Strachey, and other gentlemen took pity on Hopkins, and they asked Gates to pardon him. Finally, the governor agreed.

Before long, a third rebellion was uncovered. This time, some of the men involved in the conspiracy became frightened and betrayed their fellow conspirators.

manacles (with key)

They revealed a plot to murder Gates and his allies, steal supplies from the storehouse, and set up a permanent colony in Bermuda. According to the accusers, conspirators were scattered among both the settlement on St. George's Island and Somers's shipbuilding operation on the large island.

Now the governor wasn't sure who could be trusted. He ordered all of the settlers to carry weapons to defend themselves, and he doubled the guard.

On March 13, 1610, a gentleman named Henry Paine refused to take his watch, got into a scuffle with the guard, and swore at the commander. Paine was brought before the whole company on St. George's Island, and Gates condemned him to be hanged for treason. As the guard began to build a gallows, Paine confessed to organizing the third rebellion. Paine requested that, since he was a gentleman, his execution be carried out by gunshot, rather than by hanging. His request was granted, and he was shot to death that evening.

By the following Sunday, news of Paine's execution had reached Admiral Somers and the shipbuilders on the large island. Some of these workers had, indeed, been part of Paine's rebellion, and they were afraid that he had named them in his confession. To avoid arrest, they fled into the woods. From their hideout, they sent a petition asking Governor Gates to allow them to remain in Bermuda. They also requested a supply of clothing and a year's supply of grain.

The Mayflower II, Plymouth, MA

©Plimoth Plantation, Plymouth, Massachusetts
www.plimoth.org

## Stephen Hopkins, Colonist

Stephen Hopkins continued to play an interesting role in colonial history. After living as a castaway in Bermuda, he stayed briefly in Jamestown before returning to England. When the *Mayflower* sailed for North America in 1620, Stephen, his wife, and their children were on board. They landed at New England, along with the Pilgrims who started the Plymouth Plantation.

Gates responded by letter. He said there was enough room on the two new ships for the whole party, and that their duty was to restock Jamestown, not to start a permanent colony on Bermuda. As loyal subjects of the King, and loyal followers of Admiral Somers, Gates stated that the men must fulfill what they had set out to do.

Gates sent this letter to Somers, his friend and fellow leader. Gates asked Somers to find the deserters and convince them to rejoin the company. Somers did, and all but two of his men agreed to return. The two who remained in hiding were Christopher Carter and Robert Waters.

Certainly these crimes disturbed their small community, but the settlers also celebrated several joyous events during the winter of 1610: One couple got married and two babies were born.

Thomas Powell, who was Admiral Somers's cook, married a young woman

## Mistress Horton's Husband

Mistress Horton's husband became one of the most famous of the settlers. His name was John Rolfe. After the castaways finally reached Virginia, Mistress Horton died, and Rolfe settled in Jamestown and grew prosperous as a tobacco planter. He married one of the most well-known figures from the colonial period: the Indian maiden, Pocahontas.

Pocahontas

Photograph of a painting in the United States Capitol, copied from original by William Sheppard, dated 1616, at Barton rectory, Norfolk, England. [Library of Congress reproduction number LC-D416-18753 DLC]

named Elizabeth Persons. Elizabeth worked as the maidservant of Mistress Horton, wife of John Rolfe.

Mistress Horton also brought joy to the settlers. In February, she gave birth to the first English child born on Bermuda. (Unfortunately, the baby girl, who was named Bermuda, did not live long. She became the first infant to die on the island, as well.)

Another baby was born at the end of March, and this infant boy, Bermudas Eason, survived.

By February, berry season in Bermuda had ended. The settlers no longer had a food supply for their penned hogs, and the animals grew thin. So the men slaughtered them and salted down the meat.

Just as the hogs were getting thin, sea turtles began swimming to shore. These huge reptiles dug holes in the sand to deposit bushels of eggs. Jourdain wrote that the turtles' meat was as delicious as its eggs, and the animals produced a quantity of oil "as sweet as any butter." A single turtle fed at least fifty men, and the turtles were so plentiful that forty could be gathered in a day. Once again, Bermuda's resources amply supplied the castaways' needs.

Sea turtle

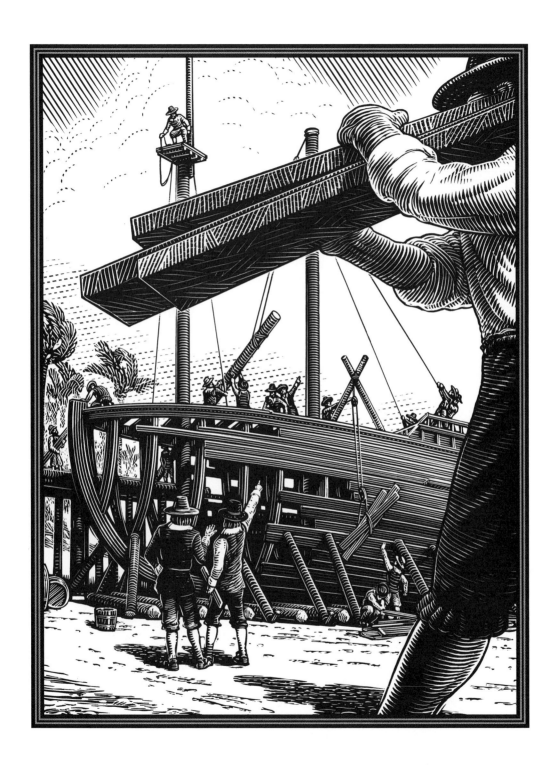

# Ships to the Sea

At the end of February, Furbusher's ship, the *Deliverance*, was assembled. It was smaller than the *Sea Venture*, measuring less than half of the wrecked ship's length, and it could carry less than one-third of the volume of cargo. The beams of the new ship were made of oak that had been stripped from the *Sea Venture*. Some of the planking that covered its ribs was also made with wood salvaged from the wreck. The rest came from Bermuda's cedar trees.

Furbusher's workers began to fill in the cracks between the new ship's planks with oakum made from old ropes. The men coated the bottom of the new ship with pitch and tar that had been salvaged from the wreck. When they ran out of this coating, they improvised another sealer by mixing whelk shells, crushed stone, turtle oil, and water.

On Friday, March 30, 1610, the men towed the *Deliverance* out of the bay and tried sailing her. She nearly capsized in the wind, so sailors carried aboard stones to weight the hold and give her balance. Once again, they tried sailing her, this time to a small island. To Sir Thomas Gates's delight, she handled well.

A month later, Admiral Somers sailed his smaller ship, the *Patience*, into the channel. The settlers knew their stay on Bermuda was almost at an end. They began to pack their clothing, blankets, and tools. They loaded salted pork, casks of fresh water, and other provisions aboard the two ships.

Gates erected a memorial of their ten-month stay on Bermuda: a cross that was screwed onto a sturdy cedar stump. The cross was made of timber salvaged from the *Sea Venture*. He fastened a silver coin, stamped with the portrait of the King of England, in the center of the cross. He engraved an inscription in copper, written in both English and Latin. It began:

> *In memory of our great deliverance, both from a mighty storm and leak, we have set up this to the honor of God. It is the spoil of an English ship...called the Sea Venture, bound...to Virginia....*

front          back

Replica of a silver coin of that era

With two new ships riding at anchor, their belongings packed, and provisions for a several-week voyage gathered, the settlers waited for a favorable wind to blow. On May 10, 1610, the wind turned westerly. Early that morning, Admiral Somers and Captain Newport set out in rowboats to mark the narrow channel with buoys to prevent their sailing ships from scraping against the reefs as they sailed out to sea.

With Somers and Newport back aboard, the ships set sail around ten in the morning. They were making their way carefully through the marked channel when the passengers and crew heard a sickening sound—the *Deliverance* struck a rock! For the next few minutes, everyone must have stood in horrified silence, waiting to hear the rush of water into the ship's torn hull. Fortunately, the sound never came. The *Deliverance* glided over the rock. The ships continued through the narrow channel without any further incidents.

For the next seven days, the two ships sailed through calm, open waters. The *Patience* could not travel as fast as the *Deliverance*, so sailors aboard the larger ship took in sails to slow its speed and keep the smaller vessel in sight.

On May 17th, sailors noticed a change in the color of the water, and they spotted debris floating by. The next day, they began to take soundings of the ocean depth. Around midnight on the twentieth of May, "we had a marvelous sweet smell from the shore," reported Strachey. At daybreak on May 21, 1610, a sailor spotted land.

Later that day, the ships rounded Cape Henry and entered Chesapeake Bay, heading for the mouth of the James River. When they were within two

miles of the fort at Point Comfort, the newcomers were greeted by a warning shot from the guard.

Admiral Somers immediately ordered the sailors to let down the anchors. Sailors lowered the rowboat and rowed to the fort to inform the guard that friendly English vessels were approaching.

The sailors who had been sent ashore soon returned with amazing news: In spite of the hurricane, most of the fleet that had traveled with the *Sea Venture* had arrived safely in Jamestown! Only one ship was lost: the small pinnace that had been towed behind the *Sea Venture*. Henry Ravens's longboat from Bermuda had not been seen. (Later, Jamestown settlers heard a rumor about the fate of this boat: The chief of the Powhatan Indians claimed that Ravens's boat reached Chesapeake Bay, wandered up the wrong river, and was ambushed by natives.)

The other news was most distressing: Jamestown was in desperate trouble. Indian attacks had been relentless, and most of the colonists had died from starvation and disease during the previous winter.

The *Deliverance* and *Patience* sailed through a thunderstorm and reached the settlement on May 23, 1610. Jamestown looked awful. Some of the palisades surrounding the town had been torn down, and the gates hung off their hinges. The settlers' houses were falling to ruin. Many houses had been stripped for firewood after their residents had died. The charred remains of buildings lay scattered within the fort.

Gates led his party ashore. They entered the town church and rang the bell to call the colonists to assemble. The newcomers watched in horror as Jamestown's skinny, ragged colonists stumbled into church. Only about sixty colonists had survived "The Starving Time," as they called the previous winter

in Jamestown. The rest had died of starvation, disease, and Indian attacks—including many of those who had been aboard the other ships in the *Sea Venture*'s fleet.

The newcomers found Jamestown's survivors so weak and demoralized that they were afraid to leave the town's palisades for fear of the Indians. The survivors had abandoned most of their efforts to produce food for themselves. They were merely waiting—for a supply ship or for death, whichever arrived first.

Master Bucke, the *Sea Venture*'s minister, held a short service. His prayers were full of sorrow for the sufferings of the Virginia colonists.

During the service, dizzying thoughts must have been running through the minds of the newcomers. For the first time, they understood that the awful hurricane and shipwreck had actually saved their lives! If they had arrived with the other ships in their fleet, they would have been forced to endure Jamestown's "Starving Time," perhaps also to die of disease, starvation, or attack. The newcomers must have wished they had remained in Bermuda, where food was plentiful and no natives threatened their safety. They realized they had sailed away from their island paradise and now faced a grim future.

After the service, Strachey read aloud the documents naming Sir Thomas Gates the new governor of the Jamestown colony (see below). Captain Percy, who had been the colony's president, handed over the council seal.

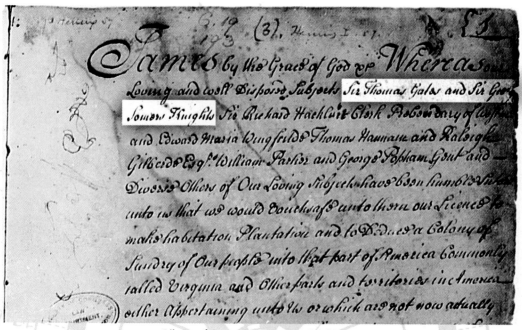

Library of Congress, Manuscript Division

Governor Gates made a speech. He announced that the provisions aboard his two ships would be shared equally among all of the colonists, old and new. Unfortunately, few provisions were left. Not realizing the desperate situation in Jamestown, his party had only brought enough food for their voyage.

Gates also promised that the colonists would not endure such awful suffering again. If a supply ship from England did not arrive soon and if they could not find a reliable source of food, Gates declared he would lead them back to England. At this, the whole assembly shouted for joy.

In the following weeks, conditions at Jamestown improved very little. Even with able-bodied newcomers at work, food remained scarce. The Indians refused to trade. Gates kept his promise. On June 7th, the Englishmen abandoned Jamestown. After crowding onto four pinnaces, they set sail. Gates planned to head up the coast to Newfoundland, where an English outpost was located. Then, as soon as they could gather enough provisions for an ocean crossing, they would set sail for England.

Lord De La Warr

But when their fleet was halfway down the James River, they were met by a rowboat of Englishmen. These messengers carried momentous news: Lord De La Warr, with three well-stocked ships, had just arrived from England. The Jamestown colony was saved!

Recovered *Sea Venture* pottery

©Dr. Jonathan Adams/Sea Venture Trust

# Legacies of the Sea Venture

When the *Deliverance* and *Patience* left Bermuda, two Englishmen were not on board: Christopher Carter and Robert Waters. These men did not want to leave the islands, fearing they would have to face punishment for their rebellion. To keep from being forced to leave, they hid in the woods.

They were not alone for long. Soon after Lord De La Warr arrived in Jamestown, Admiral Somers volunteered to lead an expedition to Bermuda to bring back provisions. On the way, Somers encountered difficult winds and fog, and his companion ship turned back.

Somers did reach Bermuda, but, having been weakened by the strenuous voyage, he died on the islands. His shipmates cut out his heart and buried it in what is now called Somers Garden in the city of St. George.

Marker where Somers' heart is buried

Leaving his heart on the islands probably would have pleased George Somers. He had fallen in love with the place and had hoped to start a plantation there someday. Somers had taken his nephew, Captain Matthew Somers, with him on the ship from Jamestown. Before his death, Somers had asked Matthew to promise that he would complete their mission and return to Virginia with supplies. Matthew ignored the promise and sailed for England instead. On the ship, he carried the preserved body of his uncle for burial in England.

One fellow from Somers's crew, Edward Chard, remained in Bermuda. For the next two years, Chard, Carter, and Waters were the only people on the islands. Then, in 1612, a ship named the *Plough* arrived from England to start a colony.

# Shakespeare and the Sea Venture

The wreck of the *Sea Venture* made a lasting impression on Bermuda's history. It also made a lasting impact on world literature. Sylvester Jourdain's report was originally published in England in 1610. William Strachey's account was not published until 1625, but it was probably circulated before that time among his friends who were writers and performers in London. Stories about the fearsome hurricane and the castaways' life on Bermuda became popular reading in England.

William Shakespeare, one of the greatest English writers, heard the story. He used it as the basis for one of his best-known plays, *The Tempest*. (A tempest is a violent storm with strong winds.)

Shakespeare

Library of Congress, Prints & Photographs Division, Theodor Horydczak Collection, [reproduction number LC-H824-T01-0016 DLC]

*The Tempest* was first performed in 1611. Many details from the play echo the castaways' experiences, including a powerful hurricane scene, spirits that supposedly haunted the islands, disagreements among the settlers, and finally, reconciliation and rescue.

# Remains of the Sea Venture

Diver Edmund Downing found the wrecked *Sea Venture* in 1958, almost 350 years after the ship went down. With government support, treasure diver E.B. "Teddy" Tucker began excavating the site in 1959. Tucker's crew brought up one of the ship's cannons and sent a photograph of it to the Tower of London for dating. The cannon was mistakenly identified as having been cast in the eighteenth century. Since the *Sea Venture* sailed from England in the early seventeenth century, this information convinced authorities that Downing had found another wrecked ship, not the *Sea Venture*. All work on the project was halted.

Almost twenty years later, in 1978, diver and historian Allan "Smokey" Wingood resumed the operation. He was joined by marine archaeologist Jonathan Adams, who had worked on the famous wreck of the *Mary Rose*, a ship sunk in 1545 off

Portsmouth in England. These men proved that the cannon had been misidentified. With better tools for recovery and dating, they established that Downing's discovery was indeed the *Sea Venture*, Bermuda's most famous shipwreck!

Over the next few years, their team measured, photographed, and made drawings of the ship's timbers as they lay on the ocean sand. The timbers are old and heavy, so no attempt was made to raise them. But Wingood and Adams did recover artifacts from the wreck: pottery, ammunition, metal weights, tobacco pipes, a dagger, a padlock, and more. Of all the objects found lying in the sand, one was particularly interesting—a candlestick that still contained a bit of candle wax. Perhaps this candlestick was dropped during the frantic search for the ship's leak. These artifacts remind tourists of the dramatic beginning of Bermuda's history. They are housed in Bermuda's Maritime Museum on Ireland Island (at the "point" of the fish-hook).

## England's Oldest Colony

Since the *Sea Venture* wrecked on its shore, Bermuda has been home to Englishmen. The nation was granted self-rule in 1968. Today Bermuda has its own constitution and prime minister, but it keeps some links with its mother country, such as its system of defense. Bermuda also has a good relationship with the United States, which operated a naval base there until 1995. Bermuda's currency is pegged to the U.S. dollar, and U.S. money is used interchangeably with Bermuda's own.

Castaways from the *Sea Venture* would scarcely recognize the islands

today. Some 60,000 people now call Bermuda home. With only twenty square miles of land, Bermuda has become one of the most densely populated places on earth. Drawn by the beauty of the place, thousands of tourists visit each year, most of them from the United States. As the country has become more urbanized, its natural environment has become threatened. Nearly one-seventh of the land is now covered with concrete.

Bermuda's plants and animals have changed radically since 1610. Most of the cedar trees have disappeared, killed by the accidental introduction of a scale insect disease in 1945. Palmettos are rare, having been intensively harvested for food and thatching materials. Tourists rave about Bermuda's gorgeous flowers, such as the hibiscus, whose blooms grow as large as saucers, the cream-colored Easter lilies, bright oleanders, and the striking blooms of the birds-of-paradise. But none of these flowers are native to the islands.

Bananas and sweet onions thrive in Bermuda's climate. In fact, the first bananas sold in London came from Bermuda. The Bermuda onion has become so famous that islanders casually refer to themselves as "Onions." Neither of these crops are native to Bermuda; they were introduced to the islands in the early seventeenth century. In fact, people have introduced so many types of plants that ninety-five percent of the country's foliage is now non-native species.

Bermuda onion

The plants that originally grew on Bermuda must be carefully nurtured today so they are not crowded out by the foreign species.

Bermuda's birds also have been affected by the islands' human population. Only three land bird species—the vireo, eastern bluebird, and catbird—have survived the changes. The arrival of other birds, such as the cardinal, goldfinch, mourning dove, starling, sparrow, pigeon, and kiskadee, are the result of the islands' changed habitat.

Vireo with chicks

Many of the sea birds that once nested all over Bermuda are struggling to survive. Shearwaters, whose haunting whistles gave the place its fearsome reputation, had vanished completely from this location by 1985. The cahow, a species that is not found anywhere else, was already in the process of disappearing when the *Sea Venture* landed, thanks to the hogs introduced by passing ships. These birds were so easily captured that laws to protect them were passed as early as 1616. Over the years, the cahows' numbers continued to decline until people assumed they were extinct. Surprisingly, in 1906, some people reported seeing cahows. A half-century later, a few of the birds were found nesting in cliff holes on Bermuda's small islets. Today several hundred breeding pairs make the place their home.

People have introduced many types of non-native creatures to the islands. These include insects, rats, and pets, such as cats and dogs. These animals, as well as pollutants in the air and water, have drastically altered the country's wildlife.

Bermuda's skink, or rock lizard, was its only land reptile when the *Sea Venture* wrecked in 1609. Today, they are rarely seen because they survive on only a few of Bermuda's small offshore islets where they are not threatened by cats and rats or crowded out by lizards introduced from the Caribbean islands.

Three types of marine turtles—the green turtle, the hawksbill, and the loggerhead—once nested on Bermuda's beaches. Jourdain wrote that there was a "great store" of these turtles, and he described how delicious their meat, oil, and eggs were. Not surprisingly, all of the sea turtles' breeding populations disappeared from the islands during the colonial period.

Today, Bermuda is very different from the place where the shipwrecked survivors of the *Sea Venture* found refuge from a deadly storm. The miracle that saved their lives resulted in the transformation of this slender chain of islands into a bustling, populated country and a famous vacation destination. Each year, tourists learn about Bermuda's history as they view artifacts from the wreck at island museums. Bermudians are proud that their country's unusual origin is immortalized in great literature—offering proof that miracles can happen and that history is sometimes stranger than fiction!

# Bibliography

## BOOKS AND MAGAZINES

Andrews, K.R. "Christopher Newport of Limehouse, Mariner." *William and Mary Quarterly.* January 1954. Volume II, Number One, pp. 28-41.

Baron, Stanley. *Your Guide to Bermuda.* London: Alvin Redman, 1965.

Bass, George F., ed. *Ships and Shipwrecks of the Americas; A History Based on Underwater Archaeology.* London: Thames and Hudson, Ltd., 1988.

Bermuda Department of Tourism. *Bermuda East to West.* Bermuda: Island Press, Ltd., October 2003.

Bermuda Zoological Society. "Bermuda's Terrestrial Fauna." Eco File, 1996.

Bermuda Zoological Society. *The Bermuda Forests.* Project Nature: 2002.

Bermuda Zoological Society. *The Rocky Coast.* [n.d.]

Darrell, Owen H. *Sir George Somers: Links Bermuda with Lyme Regis.* Hamilton: Print Express: 1997.

Glasspool, Anne. *A Summary of the Bermuda Biodiversity Strategy and Action Plan: A Blueprint for Conservation in Bermuda.* Bermuda Blueprinting, Ltd., 2003.

Godet, Theodore L. *Bermuda: Its History, Geology, Climate, Products, Agriculture, Commerce, and Government from the Earliest Period to the Present Time, with Hints to Invalids.* London: Smith, Elder & Co., 1860.

Haile, Edward Wright, ed. *Jamestown Narratives: Eyewitness Accounts of the Virginia Colony. The First Decade: 1607-1617.* Champlain, VA: Roundhouse, 1998.

Ives, Vernon A, ed. *The Rich Papers: Letters from Bermuda, 1615-1646.* Toronto, Buffalo, London: Bermuda National Trust, 1984.

Jourdain, Sylvester. *A Discovery of the Bermudas.* New York: Scholars' Facsimiles & Reprints, 1940.

Kemp, Peter, ed. *The Oxford Companion to Ships and the Sea.* Oxford, New York, Melbourne: Oxford University Press: 1976.

*Loan Exhibition of Portraits.* Hamilton: Bermuda Historical Society, 1935.

Mowbray, Louis S. *A Guide to the Reef Shore and Game Fish of Bermuda.* Bermuda: Island Press, Ltd., 1991.

Peterson, M.L.R. *"The Sea Venture." Mariner's Mirror.* 74.1. February 1988.

Porter, Darwin and Danforth Prince. *Frommer's Bermuda 2004.* New Jersey: Wiley Publishing, Inc., 2003.

*Sporty Little Field Guide to Bermuda.* 2 Halves Publishing, 1997.

Sterrer, Wolfgang, Stuart Hayward, and Vicki Gomez, eds. *Bermuda's Delicate Balance; People and the Environment.* London: Bermuda National Trust, 1982.

Sterrer, Wolfgang and A. Ralph Cavaliere. *Bermuda's Seashore Plants and Seaweeds.* Bermuda Zoological Society, 1998.

Sterrer, Wolfgang. *Marine Fauna and Flora of Bermuda; A Systematic Guide to the Identification of Marine Organisms.* New York: John Wiley, 1986.

Strode, Hudson. *The Story of Bermuda.* New York: Harcourt Brace & Co., 1932, 1946.

Tucker, Terry. *Rendezvous with Destiny: A Play in Three Scenes.* Hamilton: The Bermuda Historical Society, 1958.

Watson, J.W., J. Oliver, and C.H. Foggo. *A Geography of Bermuda.*

Wingate, David. "Breeding Birds of Bermuda." *Bermuda Environmental Studies.* Bermuda Department of Education, 1995.

Wingood, Allan J. *"Sea Venture.* An Interim Report on an Early 17th Century Shipwreck Lost in 1609." *The International Journal of Nautical Archaeology and Underwater Exploration.* 11.4, 1982.

Wingood, Allan J. with Peggy Wingood. *"Sea Venture:* The Adventure That Started 375 Years Ago." *Bermuda's Heritage, 1609-1984.* The 375th Anniversary Commemorative Edition.

Wingood, Allan J., Peggy Wingood, Jonathan Adams. Sea Venture, *The Tempest Wreck.* Bermuda: The Island Press Ltd., 1986 for the *Sea Venture* Trust.

Wright, Louis B., ed. *A Voyage to Virginia in 1609.* Charlottesville, Virginia: The University Press of Virginia, 1964.

Zuill, W.S. *The Story of Bermuda and Her People.* New York: Macmillan, 1973.

## WEBSITES

"Admiral Sir George Somers Colonized Bermuda for Britain." www.bermuda-online.org.

"Bermuda Climate, Hurricanes, and Weather" www.bermuda-online.org.

"History of Bermuda in Old and New Worlds from 1500." www.bermuda-online.org.

"Bermuda History." www.insiders.com.

Hume, Ivor Noel. "Wreck and Redemption, The *Sea Venture* Saga." www.theweboftime.com.

"*Sea Venture,* The." www.rootsweb.com/~bmuwgw/seaventure.htm

Wiley, John W. "Captain Christopher Newport." www.cnu.edu/library/Newport.html

# Index